WHY I BELONG

by Clyde H. Reid

Illustrated by Robert J. Hanson

UNITED CHURCH PRESS

BOSTON • PHILADELPHIA

KEY TO PRONUNCIATION

ă as in sat	ē as in meet	o͞o as in pool
ä as in calm	ĭ as in sit	ŭ as in up
ā as in made	ī as in kite	ū as in rule
à as in arise	ŏ as in on	û as in urge
ĕ as in set	ō as in more	

PHOTOGRAPHS: Jerome Halberstadt, pages 5, 59
H. Armstrong Roberts, page 87
Peter C. Schlaifer, page 81
Joe Tritsch, pages iv, 68
Wide World Photos, pages 11, 35

Scripture quotations, unless otherwise indicated, are from the *Revised Standard Version of the Bible,* copyrighted 1946 and 1952 by the Division of Christian Education, National Council of Churches, and are used by permission.

This book is part of the United Church Curriculum, prepared and published by the Division of Christian Education and the Division of Publication of the United Church Board for Homeland Ministries.

Library of Congress Catalog Card Number 64–19461

Contents

About This Book 1

Attack on Delinquency: Sylvester Fields 3

"Thank God I Am Alive": William McCormack 9

John F. Kennedy 13

"Who Will Do This?": McDonald Major 15

A Growing Faith: Laura Jean Mashrick 19

A Pilot Speaks: William D. Short 23

Water-Poured-on-My-Head: John Stacy 27

Martin Luther King, Jr. 31

To Jail for Freedom: Pauline Knight 33

At the Gas Pump: Rex Jordan 39

In Devil's Well Hollow: Lillian Wallace 43

Filled with Joy: Samuel Devapragasam 47

Dr. Rice Speaking: Dr. Glen Rice 51

Adlai E. Stevenson 55

"Why Aren't You Hip?": Raymond Rodriguez ... 57

Alive Today: Soshichiro Sasaki 61

Lyndon B. Johnson 65

View from a Bus: William H. Glaser 67

Talent to Bring Joy: Jimilu Mason 71

Dwight D. Eisenhower 77

Doctor on Horseback: Dr. William L. Nute, Sr. ... 79

The Gift of God: Harold Goldthwaite 85

Where You Find God: Albert Jenkins 89

Footnotes and Acknowledgments 92

About This Book

In this book all kinds of people—Christians from many places and many walks of life—describe what belonging to the church means to them. You will hear from a farmer, a doctor, and a sculptor. You will read about some people who are educated and others who are not. You have never heard of many of these Christians, but some are well-known, even famous. They are real people; they told their stories to me, and I have written them down for you.

The church means many different things to these Christians. Each has caught hold of part of the wonder of belonging to the fellowship of those who know Jesus Christ as Lord. No one knows the full meaning of belonging to Christ's church, but what these people say may give you some clues about what it may mean for you to say, "I belong to the church of Jesus Christ."

1

SYLVESTER FIELDS grew up in the Bedford-Stuyvesant area
of Brooklyn. He worked with young people of the area
for the Nazarene Congregational Church

Attack on Delinquency

Over in one corner of the school playground five or six teenage boys were huddled in a tight circle. It was a typical summer day, and the playground was crowded with young people. I walked slowly up to the boys and said, "Hi, fellows."

Someone quickly picked up the dice, and the money on the ground disappeared like magic. I heard someone say, "Let's shove off, man." They gave me dirty looks and drifted slowly off. I walked on across the playground and joined some boys playing basketball. While we stopped for time out, I got acquainted with several of them.

"You guys live around here?"

"Yah, over on Hancock Street."

"My name's Syl. What's yours?"

"I'm Jim and this is Ed."

I put out my hand and we shook.

My job was unusual. I was called a street worker. It was my business to get acquainted with young people in the neighborhood and help them in any way I could. So I made contacts with them where they were—in a crap game, on the basketball court, in the pool hall, at the corner store. I was not an ordained minister, but I worked for the Nazarene Congregational Church in Brooklyn.

Within a mile of the church were about five thousand teenagers with little or no church background. My job was to work with these young people in limbo—teenagers who had no champion, no cause, no recognition, no purpose.

I helped them find part-time jobs, encouraged them to finish school, and counseled with them when they got into trouble. I guided some of them into classes at our church where they could learn to read, for many of them had never learned. Mostly, I tried to be their friend. At the church we called this our "frontal attack on delinquency."

To make this job easier we established a teen center called "Halfway House." The center was located in a former beauty parlor on a corner several blocks from the church. The center had recreation rooms and counseling offices.

I remember when we were painting and fixing the place up. I was up on a ladder when I noticed several boys about fourteen or fifteen years old outside the door. I recognized them as members of a local gang and went out to talk with them. Several of them had been drinking. I could tell they were interested in the center, but they acted as though they didn't care. I had talked with one or two of them on a playground or somewhere before. I told them I could use some help fixing up the floors, painting, and so on. They agreed to come back later to help, and several of them did come and work at the center. This way a friendship began.

The Nazarene Congregational Church is located in the Bedford-Stuyvesant area of Brooklyn, a neighborhood with a bad reputation. Thirty years before it had been mostly a white neighborhood. Now it was largely Negro and Puerto Rican, although a good many white people remained. Because of overcrowded housing and lowered morale in the community, there were gangs of delinquents. Occasionally gang rivalries erupted into "rumbles" or fights.

In trying to reach out to the needs of this area, the Nazarene Congregational Church launched an exciting program. My job as street worker was part of that program. Besides the regular minister, we also had a minister from Puerto Rico who worked with the people who spoke Spanish. We needed another staff member to help people with their housing problems and work for better housing in the area. But there was not enough money. Many times landlords took advantage of the people and cheated them badly.

I knew the problems of the Bedford-Stuyvesant area because I had grown up and lived there most of my life. I went to Long Island University where I was on the basketball and track teams. While I was in the army I helped organize a basketball team that won many games and was asked to tour Europe and the Middle East. I was also named to the all-star football team of our army command. All this background helped me understand and work with the teenagers of the Bedford-Stuyvesant area.

One night, at about 11:45 P.M., my phone rang at home. One of the boys in our church—let's call him Tom—a high school senior, was missing. Tom had not gone to his after-school job that day, and his friends had not seen him at school.

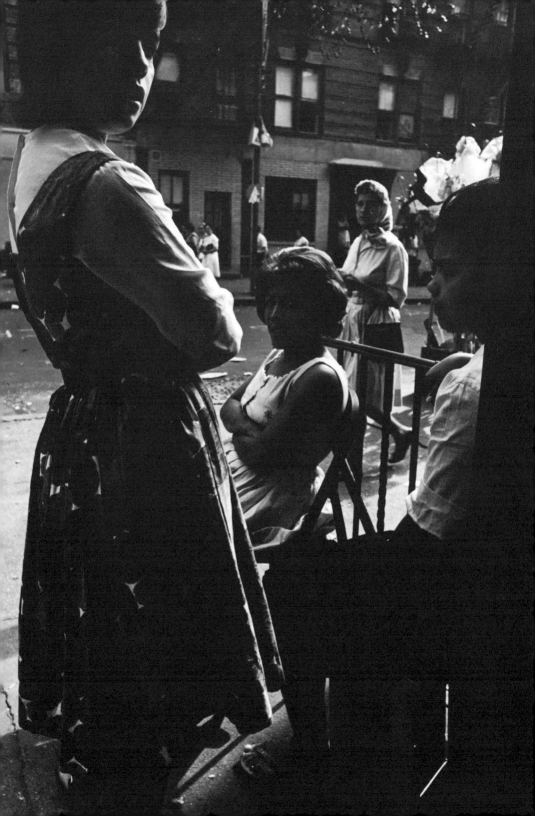

I started out to see if I could find him. I checked the local police stations, but he was not there, and the police had no information on him. I walked the streets in the area. No sign of Tom. I took a subway to downtown New York City and watched to see if he would come out of a late movie in Times Square. I couldn't find him.

Early the next morning Tom phoned me. He said that he was in Michigan, had a full-time job as a shipping clerk, and would be all right. I thought his story sounded fishy, and after a long conversation I learned that he was not in Michigan at all. He was right in New York City, not too far away. He was really running away from a problem with his father at home.

I finally persuaded Tom to come back home and finish school. I promised to help him work things out with his father. I got only one hour of sleep out of twenty-four that day. Six weeks later Tom graduated from high school, very grateful that he had finished. He soon entered the armed forces.

I remember one particular girl I worked with. Let's call her Julie. She came from a broken home and was a real tomboy. There was no one—boy or girl—whom she would not fight. She was also the leader of a small band of girls. Once Julie was escorted from our "Teen Church" service for losing her temper, cursing out loud, and making off-color remarks.

Once I asked her, "What do you girls do at your club meetings?" She replied that they prayed sometimes.

"What do you pray for?"

"We pray that each girl can learn to do her part in a fight. We also make rules for fighting, like if some other girl is fighting one of our girls in a fair fight we don't jump in unless our girl is getting beat up."

"What else do you do at your meetings?"

"We read the Bible."

"How?"

"Well, someone will read something and the other girls will ask if she understands it. If she says yes we read something else."

"Who leads the discussion?"

"First one, then the other."

6

"How old is the oldest girl?"

"Fourteen."

"Do you ask any adults to help in the reading and discussion?"

"No."

"Do you girls smoke?"

"Who don't?"

"When you pray, do you ask God to help you to be good girls?"

"No, we pray that we don't chicken out in a fight."

We talked some more. Three weeks later, Julie came up to me and said, "Mr. Fields, if I start to change my friends and stay out of fights, do you think you could find me a job where I could meet some nice people?"

In big, crowded cities like New York, Chicago, and Los Angeles, there are many opportunities to help people like Tom and Julie. As a Christian, I'm glad I could serve my church in this way.

WILLIAM McCORMACK, an officer in the St. Louis Police Department, belongs to the Nazareth United Church of Christ in St. Louis

"Thank God I Am Alive"

It was a rainy afternoon in October. About 3 P.M. the call came over the radio in the squad car in which my partner and I were riding. A man carrying several loaded guns had been seen hopping a freight train coming in our direction. He must have been insane with hate. He had said that he would kill any policeman he saw.

We raced toward the railroad yard. As a train approached, we crossed a viaduct over the tracks and spotted the armed man in a coal car. We signaled the engineer and he stopped the train. My partner and I radioed headquarters that we had found the man and described the location. Immediately other cars were dispatched to our aid. We proceeded to the railroad yard. As we climbed out of the car, we each said a prayer asking God to watch over us. My partner was Catholic and he made the sign of the cross.

The coal car was about two hundred feet away. I approached it from the front, while my partner went around the other side. When I was about seventy-five feet from the man, I started talking to him, hoping he would not notice my partner approaching from the rear. The man shouted at me and told me not to came any closer or he would shoot. I kept on talking, thinking he would give up. Suddenly he saw some other policemen arriving and became panicky. Raising his gun to his shoulder he fired. I heard the bullet from his deer rifle whiz past my left ear. A few inches difference and I would have been killed. Minutes later the man was captured, and I breathed a sigh of relief. At the supper table with my family that night, we gave thanks to God that I was still alive.

I was raised in a very tough neighborhood in the northern part of St. Louis. The kids had to play in the streets because we had no playgrounds. My mother was Protestant, but my father was Roman Catholic so I belonged to his church and went to a Catholic school. Later when I was living with an aunt in another city, I went to a Protestant Sunday School and became a Protestant. The church I joined was very strict about some things. At one time I joined a lodge, and the church told me I had to resign. I refused. They told me that I would be expelled from the church if I didn't resign from the lodge. I still refused; so they expelled me.

One day later on I was talking to my sergeant on the force, and asked him about his church. I wanted my family to have a place to worship, and I wanted my boy to grow up in the Christian faith. The sergeant invited me and my family to his church, the Nazareth Evangelical and Reformed Church. We have been active in that church ever since.

Being a Christian policeman does make a difference. As I patrol my beat, I tell people about my church. I try to get them to become active in their own churches. Occasionally, someone tries to bribe me. When I remind them that I am a Christian, they usually give up the attempt.

The beat that I walk in St. Louis is a very busy territory. I meet all kinds of people. Some of them are running away from themselves and God. I remember one man I found sitting on a bench across from the railroad station. When I approached him he started to get up and leave.

"Don't go away," I said. "I'd like to talk to you for a minute." I asked him if he ever went to church.

"Oh, yah, I used to go to church before I started drinking."

Then he told me the story of his troubled life. He had been a lieutenant in the fire department. He was highly educated, had a wonderful wife and two girls, and had owned his own home. After he began drinking his wife left him, and he wound up on Market Street where the drunkards hang out.

I asked him why he didn't go back to church and try to start life anew.

"Naw, I just couldn't go to church the way I feel. I'm not in the right frame of mind to go to church," he answered.

I ignored his misunderstanding of how willing the church is to accept people. Instead, I said, "Look, I have another idea. Why don't you get out of St. Louis. Go to another city where nobody knows you and start all over. You could get a job, join a church of your faith, and make a new beginning. I'm sure of one thing— God will help you if you ask him."

I left him sitting and thinking.

I love to talk to people and listen to their troubles. When they ask my advice I try to help them. I usually tell them to pray. I think that is the best way to handle problems. Take your trouble to God and he will help you.

In my youth I was a wrestler, a track man, and a good swimmer. I also belonged to the St. Louis Rowing Club. Now I do a little fishing. And I do a lot of fishing for men—for the church.

I belong to the church because it gives me a better outlook on life in these troubled times. It gives me spiritual guidance and confidence in myself. It is great to be where I can pray and worship the way I want to. Being a good Christian gives me strength in myself, and helps me be the backbone of my family and my church.

John F. Kennedy, President of the
United States, 1961–1963

In the long history of the world, only a few generations have been granted the role of defending freedom in its hour of maximum danger. I do not shrink from this responsibility—I welcome it. I do not believe that any of us would exchange places with any other people or any other generation. The energy, the faith, the devotion which we bring to this endeavor will light our country and all who serve it—and the glow from that fire can truly light the world.

And so, my fellow Americans: ask not what your country can do for you—ask what you can do for your country.

My fellow citizens of the world: ask not what America will do for you, but what together we can do for the freedom of man.

Finally, whether you are citizens of America or citizens of the world, ask of us here the same high standards of strength and sacrifice which we ask of you. With a good conscience our only sure reward, with history the final judge of our deeds, let us go forth to lead the land we love, asking His blessing and His help, but knowing that here on earth God's work must truly be our own.

—from his Inaugural Address,
January 20, 1961

McDONALD MAJOR, a native of Southern Rhodesia, was raised and educated by the Mount Silinda mission of the United Church of Christ. He is now a teacher in Southern Rhodesia, having received his college education in the United States

"Who Will Do This?"

"Don't worry, Zondiwe. I'll protect you."

I tried to look as brave as a nine-year-old boy can look, but inside I was terrified. Night was falling rapidly, and my sister Zondiwe (zŏn-dē'wē) and I were alone in the bush. My mother had died when I was still very small, and my father had gone off to work in the mines at Johannesburg, leaving us in the care of one of his other wives. Now we had run away from our home in a little African village, feeling that we had been mistreated. In one hand I held a club, in the other a few berries I had found.

"Look, we have some supper," I said, trying to be cheerful. Somehow we survived the night, and our spirits began to rise.

For days we wandered from village to village, looking for a job and protection. Eventually we found an African businessman who needed a young boy to look after his cattle. Zondiwe was given a job in the kitchen. We were very excited and happy. For the first time since our mother had died we had enough to eat.

One day I noticed that other young people spent the morning hours in a small building. I inquired and learned that they were going to school. When I had an opportunity, I spoke to my employer, "Sir, would it be possible for me to go to school and learn, if I work very hard the rest of the day?" He agreed, and for the first time my sister and I began to go to school.

Then one day they came for us. The people in our village had learned where we were and had come to take us home. As our cart bounced back into the familiar village, the witch doctor came out angrily to meet us. He was dressed in a leopard skin and his head was covered with long feathers. He scolded me severely. He told me that I had angered the spirits by attending the white man's school. He warned me never to run away again. I was terribly frightened.

My stepmother grabbed me by the jaws, and hauling me like a lion, she threw me into the hut and barred the door. For two hours I wasn't myself. I thought of my sister and of my dead mother. What a poor and miserable picture my future presented. I tried to sleep to forget everything, but I couldn't. The image of the horrible witch doctor kept haunting me, and the idea of having angered the spirits overwhelmed me.

15

Yet, when everything looked to be at its worst, when life was no life to me, I seemed to hear a strange, faint, sweet, and loving voice calling me from a distance. I listened but did not understand. Late at night, I collected courage and decided to run away to a distant place where I would be able to hear the voice which now seemed to be my only hope. Quietly I gathered together my few belongings, got out through the roof, and ran away as fast as I could.

After wandering for several days, I came to a place where friendly people welcomed me and gave me work to do and something to eat. It was the Mount Silinda mission of the United Church of Christ. The mission included a church, schools, a large farm, and a medical clinic. People often walked long distances to reach the mission since this part of Africa had almost no religious, medical, or educational services. Mount Silinda has been serving the area since 1893.

After a few months I went to attend the service at the church, and for the first time in my life I heard of a loving Father, the father of the rich and the poor, the happy and the miserable.

At the mission I was able to continue my education. When one of my first teachers asked me what my name was, I replied, "Mahlangeni Maixeke." In my native tongue my name means the "unexpected survival of God's child."

Because I was born during a famine, my parents did not name me at first, thinking I would soon die of starvation. A year later, when I still insisted on living, they gave me my name which is difficult for English-speaking people to pronounce. When my teacher at Mount Silinda heard me say my name with a loud clacking sound, she said simply, "That won't do. What is your father's name?"

"Major Malanga," I replied.

"Your name will be McDonald Major," she said without hesitation. And so it has been ever since.

As my own education continued, I decided that what I wanted most in the world was to be a teacher. I wanted to help my fellow Africans who still lived in a world of fear and superstition. I remembered my home village and the great evergreen forest to the north. According to our people the forest was the home of ghosts, spirits, great witches, and wizards.

In fact, my people were ruled by fear. There was great fear of outside invasion. There was fear of the spirits of our ancestors, who had the secret and magic of life, and were capable of bringing prosperity or destruction to our homes. These spirits were hard to please, but easy to anger. There was great fear of breaking the tribal laws, customs, and taboos. There was great fear of famine. There was fear of wild animals. There was fear of the white man—the missionary—because the white man and his religion seemed to be against the religion of the tribe, and to be against the tribal religion would anger the spirits of our forefathers. There were many, many fears and superstitions, and I wanted to help my people to know that they did not need to fear. There is need for African teachers, but there are few African teachers available.

After several years at the Mount Silinda mission I went to a government school to study further. I became an elementary teacher, and later returned to teach eighth grade at one of the mission schools. By this time I had met Tracy and married her.

One day a great opportunity came to me. I was asked if I would like to go to America to get a college education. The American Board (forerunner of the United Church Board for World Ministries) was willing to help me because Africa needed teachers with a college education so badly. Such an opportunity comes to few Africans, and I knew how fortunate I was. However, it was very difficult to leave Tracy and our three children behind at home for four years.

I asked myself over and over, "Who will do this—leave his family for so long?" My answer each time was, "Unless I am willing I should not expect anyone else to do this for my people. I will do it!" I needed to follow Jesus and thank him for what he had done for me. It was the hardest decision of my life, but Tracy and the girls would not let me pass up this opportunity for education. So I decided, and came to America to study at Clark University in Worcester, Massachusetts.

I have always been grateful that I came to the Mount Silinda mission and learned about God and about Jesus Christ. It couldn't have been my own cleverness or wisdom or intelligence that made me escape death and that enabled me to get the same education as the rich and happy. Someone must have been looking after me.

17

LAURA JEAN MASHRICK was a secretary for the youth department of the United Church of Christ. She has since studied at Union Theological Seminary and is serving as Director of Christian Education in a church in Massachusetts

A Growing Faith

I rubbed my eyes to be sure I wasn't dreaming. As I looked around the breakfast table, I saw the faces of my new friends from Germany, Italy, Belgium, Holland, Algeria, Angola, and several other countries. I was at a work camp for young people sponsored by the World Council of Churches. We finished our simple breakfast of bread, jam, and cocoa and gathered in a quiet room of the old French house. The French Reformed Church had purchased the house as a camp for children from Paris, and our job was to help fix it up. Pierre was our worship leader that morning. During the camp we took turns leading the simple morning service. Though we came from many different backgrounds, we found much inspiration from our worship services together.

A typical day in camp began early. By 7:15 we were hard at work building a volleyball court, painting the rooms of the old house, or doing other jobs to help prepare the new camp. We stopped at 10:30 for our "second breakfast" of bread and sausage, then back to work. In France your main meal is eaten at noon, so we had our dinner at 1:30. After dinner we sometimes had discussion groups, and it was fascinating to exchange ideas with young people from so many different backgrounds. On Sundays we visited spots of historical interest, and sometimes we took a whole weekend for a longer sightseeing trip.

Through meeting, working, talking, and living with young people from different religious backgrounds, we came to understand one another as individuals, not as foreigners. Because of this experience I came to see my own country and religious beliefs in a new way. I will never forget my work camp experience.

Back home in Massachusetts I found a job. If anyone had asked me what I wanted to do when I finished college, I probably would have said, "I don't know what I want to do, but I know you'll never catch me cooped up in an office, pounding a typewriter all day."

But guess what? The job I landed was as a secretary. Not only that; I really enjoyed it. I worked for the youth department of the Division of Christian Education of the United Church of Christ. I don't know whether I would have liked being a secretary anywhere else, but I know I did like my job there: writing letters, answering requests from youth groups for materials, and learning about new ideas and plans for United Church young people.

Because I worked for the church, you probably think it was easier for me to be a Christian on the job than it is for other people. I'm not sure about that. No matter where you work you have to learn to accept other people as individuals, to overlook their habits that annoy you, and to keep from making snap judgments about them.

For instance, a few days after a new girl had come to work in our building, she came into our office and said, "How come your office was closed a while ago? I tried to get in but the door was locked."

She sounded a little impatient, and my first reaction was to say something sharp in return. After a few more days, I began to understand her better. She had not realized that we sometimes had coffee breaks, or had to run errands to the post office or the bookstore. She was uncertain about the rules, and a little scared too, just starting a new job. I realized that she had not meant to sound ill-tempered; she was just uncertain. If I had jumped to a wrong conclusion about her and said something unkind, I might have lost a friend and hurt her feelings as well.

Then, too, in my work I had to be honest with myself and my employers about the hours I kept and the amount of work I did. My boss was away much of the time, and there was no time clock to punch. If I had wanted to cheat, it would have been easy to get away with it. But, to me, being a Christian means trying to be honest with yourself and with others. I think we have to love our neighbors as ourselves not just on Sundays, but every day.

I grew up in a Congregational church in my hometown of Milton, not far from Boston. I was very active in our church youth group and was a state officer. I particularly enjoyed summer youth conferences. While I was in college, I taught church school for two years.

I belong to the church because I think that part of being a Christian is worshiping and working with other Christians. Perhaps a person can lead a good life without being a church member, but if you belong to the church you have the encouragement of other people to help you grow in the faith. Also you can do a lot more for others through the church, because it is set up to help people. I don't think the church is an organization of "good" people; it is (or should be) an organization of people who are *trying* to be good because they believe in the goodness of God.

Because the church is made up of imperfect people, it isn't perfect either. For instance, I think we in the church have to take more decisive stands on social problems like prejudice. I think churches must continue to work hard at settling their differences and cooperating in organizations such as the World Council of Churches. This can show non-Christians that Christians really do believe what they preach about.

The more I learn about my church and my faith, the more I realize how little I really know. I have often doubted my beliefs and changed them as I heard other ideas or read a new book. But I think this is healthy, and I hope that as I grow older and continue to learn, my faith will also grow.

WILLIAM D. SHORT of Lynnfield, Massachusetts, is a pilot
for American Airlines

A Pilot Speaks

As we taxied down the runway I felt good. The weather reports were encouraging. The sun was shining brightly. It was a perfect day to be captain of a big, fast, modern airliner en route from Boston to Chicago.

The powerful engines responded smoothly to the controls. The ship gained flying speed and the wheels slowly left the ground. I felt that same old thrill I always feel as a pilot. What a miracle it is to leave the ground, climb high above the earth, and see its beauty spread out below.

We gained altitude and began banking around to head west for Chicago. As I looked down I could see Boston Harbor glistening in the sun—Boston Harbor, where the Puritans had landed in their frail little ships, smaller than my airplane. I could see the slim tower of the Bunker Hill monument, where the War of Independence had begun, where men had given their lives for the right to be free. I could see the spire of Old North Church, where someone had hung a lantern and signaled Paul Revere to begin his famous midnight ride. I felt a deep pride in my country as I recalled those historic events.

As the plane slowly settled onto course I glanced off to my right. I could see the little town that I call home, where my wife and our twelve-year-old son would be waiting when my flight returned. We live in a small suburban town just north of Boston. In the next town, seven miles away, is the little Methodist church that we attend. We belong to it because we have helped build it up, and we feel at home with the people there.

I very carefully checked the instruments as the plane settled down to a steady, smooth flight. I noticed a train chugging its way out of Boston along the Charles River. It reminded me of how far I had come since the day I graduated from high school and went to work for the railroad, earning fourteen dollars a week. It was during the depression and there were five children in our family, so I could not afford to go to college. I used to spend my weekends at the local airport, working around the airplanes, selling ride tickets, and doing anything else I could find to do. I worked in trade for flying lessons. Finally, at the age of twenty-one, I got my instructor's license and could make a living flying. When the Second World War broke out I became an instructor in the United States Air Force. When I was discharged after the war, I got a job with the American Airlines as a co-pilot. I've been flying with them ever since.

The plane was flying smoothly and everything seemed under control, so I decided to take a break. I turned the controls over to my co-pilot and opened the door into the passengers' cabin. As I walked slowly down the aisle a man with a very worried look on his face leaned over and grabbed my coat sleeve.

"Are we in trouble, captain? Is there anything wrong?"

I'm always tempted to be impatient and a little angry with people like that. They upset the other passengers for no good reason. In this work I'm in contact with many people each day: the crewmen assigned to me for the flight, the agents, dispatchers, and maintenance men, the stewardesses, and most importantly, the passengers. I think it's very important to apply my Christian understanding in my work. The people who work for me have the same feelings I had when I worked for someone, and I try to put myself in their place. I try to figure out how I would like to be treated if I had the same problem and was in the same position.

So I asked myself how that passenger must feel. I decided that maybe this was his first flight, and possibly he was frightened. He needed to be reassured, not reprimanded or ignored. So I smiled and spoke so the others could hear too.

"Why, everything's just fine. I thought I'd come back and see how you folks were getting along back here. Is the stewardess taking good care of you?"

This relieved the momentary tension the passenger had created and he began to relax. I asked him if he had been on this flight before. "No," he said, "in fact this is my first ride in a plane!"

"Well, I hope you enjoy your flight," I replied and moved on down the aisle. I think consideration for others and being fair to them is something that cannot be overstressed. And I think that a person who goes to church *and listens,* and makes an effort to live as a Christian, has less trouble making the right decisions because

24

most of the time he thinks of others and what's best for everyone.

I returned to the controls. I soon noticed that the clouds were getting thicker and the weather was closing in. By the time we reached Chicago it was pretty bad. The tower signaled us to circle the city until we could find an opening in the clouds to break through. We stayed at our assigned altitude and circled the city for more than an hour. I was beginning to worry about my fuel supply when I got the signal to come on in. I breathed a silent prayer of thanks to God and we landed a few minutes later.

The rain was falling hard by the time we unloaded our passengers, and it looked as though the return flight next morning might be canceled. I realized that I could be stuck for the weekend. I mentally made plans to attend church in Chicago. Somehow worshiping with strangers isn't the same as attending your own church, where you know people and they know you, and where you can help with the work of the church in a tangible way. I attend church every Sunday I'm home, which is two or three times a month. I think it's very important to worship God in church so you can apply what you learn to your daily life. If you do unto others as you would have them do unto you, you can help make the world a better place to live in.

Early the next morning the phone in my hotel room rang, and I was glad. I knew it would be the dispatcher. Sure enough, the weather had cleared and we would be flying after all. I looked forward to getting back home, where I could be with my family and attend my own church.

JHONAKEHUNKGA, or JOHN STACY, was a beloved Christian
leader and a chief of the Winnebago Indians in Wisconsin.
He died on July 5, 1956 at the age of eighty-nine

Water-Poured-on-My-Head

My name is Jhonakehunkga. I am a Winnebago Indian chief and a Christian. I am usually known by my English name, John Stacy. You might be interested in how I received that name.

My father worked for an Irishman who could not pronounce my father's name, so he just called him "Indian." One day the Irishman asked my father why he didn't find a name that a man could pronounce.

"What's your name?" asked my father.

"Stacy," he replied.

"All right, I'll take your name," my father said.

So my father became Mike Stacy. Later he named me John Stacy, after his employer. When I was nine years old Jacob Hauser of the Reformed Church came to establish a mission in our Winnebago settlement near Black River Falls, Wisconsin. In 1878 he opened a Christian school in a little log schoolhouse we had built, and I was one of the first ten Indian children to be enrolled there.

Missionary Hauser found the Winnebago people in a sorry state, living in poverty, starvation, and sickness. For years we had been pushed from reservation to reservation as our lands were taken from us. From that humble beginning we have come a long way. Today we have several mission churches and a wonderful boarding school for children.

The missionaries were patient men. For twenty years they taught us and helped us and loved us, but not one Winnebago had become a Christian. Then one Good Friday, when I was a young man of twenty-nine, missionary Jacob Stucki read us the story of the crucifixion and asked if one of us would repeat the story in his own words.

I stood and told the crucifixion story in my own words. When I had finished, I stood silently, deep in thought. Finally with tears in my eyes I cried, "Is it possible that God can love a man like this? If it is so, then I give myself to him!" After several months of instruction, my wife, Martha and David Decorah, and I were baptized as the first Winnebago Christians of that mission.

I had the privilege of helping missionary Stucki as his lay assist-

27

ant. Together we translated part of the Bible into the Winnebago language so my people could read it for the first time. The American Bible Society published the translation for us.

When I was a young man I was well-known for my strength, although I was a short man. Wrestling is a favorite sport with the Winnebago, and I was an outstanding wrestler. When the Stucki boys were growing up, I challenged them to take me on in a wrestling match. One day Calvin Stucki, who was almost six feet tall, decided he would accept that challenge. We started to wrestle, but the match was soon over. I just picked Calvin up, doubled him up like a jackknife, tucked him under my arm, carried him out to the barn, and dumped him into a horse manger. That was the last time those boys wrestled with me.

My own people made it very difficult for me when I became a Christian. My father took my children away and would not let me see them for a long time. He said my wife and I were not fit to bring them up. Later I purchased a government homestead of 120 acres and built my own farmhouse and barn. I became the first Winnebago to own a herd of cattle. By Winnebago standards I was a prosperous man.

On one occasion I left the mission early one morning and hiked up to my farm, forty-four miles away. I finished some chores there and hiked the forty-four miles back, arriving at the mission late in the evening. When I told a white friend about this he objected. "Why, John, a man can't really *walk* that far in a day. In walking one always has one foot on the ground. You must have *run!*"

"Oh," I said, "I just lean my body forward and then, to keep it from falling, I put my foot under it, and that's the way I keep on going. I can go like that all day."

Sometimes to test me, sometimes to torment me, many people used to come to my home for a meal. I remember on some occasions as many as thirty people arrived uninvited for dinner. My wife had to cook quantities of meat and bushels of vegetables. I could have run them off, but that would have hurt the cause of Christianity. They were testing me as a Christian. I always kept silent, but after dinner no guest was allowed to leave until I had read my usual chapter from one of the Gospels and said a simple prayer.

Even though my people treated me badly for being a Christian, they honored me when they elected me to represent them in Washington, D.C. They made me a Winnebago chief for this purpose.

My wife's mother was a widow, so we took her to live with us. She was with us for twenty years until her death. She never spoke to me except to insult me, and she did everything she could to make my life miserable because of my religion. She would never eat at the same table with us, which is a great insult to a Winnebago. When we had our devotions at the table, she rattled her dishes and scolded loudly. We paid no attention. Many times she tried to poison me. For years I would eat no food unless my wife prepared it herself.

In 1930 Jacob Stucki died after many years of service to the Winnebago people. His son Benjamin took his place. One day "Mr. Ben" was visiting in my home, and my mother-in-law "bawled out" my wife terribly. Mr. Ben asked me, "How can you and your wife take all that?"

I thought about it and then said, "I guess if we weren't Christians, I would have thrown her over the fence long ago."

Finally the day came when the old lady was near death. She kept calling for me, but when I came to her bedside she had nothing to say. This happened many times. Finally she spoke, "My son, many years I have hated you and despised your ways. I have spoken much evil against you and have done you much harm. I have caused you and your family much suffering. These many years I have looked upon and watched your ways. Now I know that your way is right and my way was wrong. My days are done and I shall soon die. Now I also want 'water-poured-on-my-head' [baptism]. When I die, do not let the other Indians take me away. I want you and your family to bury me in your way."

"Wogishawarnankshana naxirag wanajojaisgera, hungma wangregi herara earninege." ("Blessed are the poor in spirit, for theirs is the kingdom of heaven." Matthew 5:3, from the Winnebago Bible)

All those years of Christian patience and love really did make a difference! [1]

Martin Luther King, Jr., a Baptist minister, has become one of the foremost leaders of the nonviolent struggle of American Negroes for full freedom, justice, and equal opportunity in the United States

There was a time when the church was very powerful—in the time when the early Christians rejoiced at being deemed worthy to suffer for what they believed. In those days the church was not merely a thermometer that recorded the ideas and principles of popular opinion; it was a thermostat that transformed the mores of society. Wherever the early Christians entered a town the power structure immediately sought to convict them for being "disturbers of the peace" and "outside agitators." But the Christians pressed on, in the conviction the they were "a colony of heaven," called to obey God rather than man. Small in number, they were big in commitment. . . .

Things are different now. So often the contemporary church is a weak, ineffectual voice with an uncertain sound. So often it is an archdefender of the status quo. Far from being disturbed by the presence of the church, the power structure of the average community is consoled by the church's silent—and often even vocal—sanction of things as they are.

But the judgment of God is upon the church as never before. If today's church does not recapture the sacrificial spirit of the early church, it will lose its authenticity, forfeit the loyalty of millions, and be dismissed as an irrelevant social club with no meaning for the twentieth century. Every day I meet young people whose disappointment with the church has turned into outright disgust. . . . Perhaps I must turn my faith to the inner spiritual church, the church within the church, as the true *ecclesia* and the hope of the world.[2]

—from his "Letter from a Birmingham Jail"

PAULINE KNIGHT was a senior in college when she participated in the freedom ride she describes

To Jail for Freedom

Early on the morning of May 27, 1961, when I was a senior at Tennessee State University, I boarded a Greyhound bus in Nashville, Tennessee, with nine other students. We were bound for New Orleans by way of Alabama and Mississippi. We were determined to insist on our right to use the facilities at bus terminals in the South without being segregated into white and black groups, even if it meant going to jail.

At eight o'clock that night we reached Montgomery, Alabama, and a crowd was waiting for us. As we got off the bus and stood silently, I carefully noticed the peoples' faces. I never would have believed that people could be so filled with hate. Fortunately they did not bother us, and we went to the home of a minister where we spent the night.

At his home we were joined by a large group of other students from colleges across the country. We spent most of the night mapping our strategy. We talked about what could happen to us on the trip and what we would do if it did. As members of a nonviolent movement, we believed in using love rather than violence to overthrow injustice. This belief means that we cannot strike back even if attacked. We believe that love is the force by which God binds man to himself and man to man. Such love goes to the extreme, and it remains loving and forgiving even in the midst of hostility.

Before we retired that night, I was chosen spokesman for the group. As I lay in bed I became troubled as I suddenly realized that I would have to make decisions that would affect the whole group. I remembered what I had been taught by leaders of the nonviolent movement like the Rev. James Lawson: "You must have inner integrity: a willingness to remain on firm ground and act on impulses of love and goodwill in spite of what may happen." I then remembered this verse from Ephesians: "Therefore take the whole armor of God, that you may be able to withstand in the evil day, and having done all, to stand." (Ephesians 6:13)

The next morning as we left the house, soldiers popped up from everywhere. They followed us to the bus station where we boarded a bus for Jackson, Mississippi. People stared at us as though we were creatures from outer space. Upon our arrival in Jackson we got off the bus and went to a waiting room labeled, WHITE WAITING ROOM. A large group of people, including the police, were on hand to meet us.

When we walked into the waiting room, the police captain told us to move on. Before we had a chance to move on, however, we were arrested and taken to a police wagon bound for the city jail. Our group remained calm, and we joined in singing our nonviolent movement theme song, "We Shall Overcome."

Our trial was set for 3 P.M. the following day. We were each found guilty and sentenced to jail or to a $200 fine. We all chose going to jail in protest against the injustice of our sentence rather than paying a fine for an offense we had not committed. We were then taken to the county jail, thirty students in all. We were all happy, laughing, talking, and singing. The guards looked at us as though we were idiots. Sometimes they told us to stop singing, but we kept on. I was reminded of Dr. Martin Luther King's words, "Do what you will to us, but we will wear you down."

We were in the county jail for twenty-seven days. Conditions there were very bad. Many of us had to sleep on thin cotton mats on the floor. There were twenty of us in a cell the size of a small room. It was impossible to walk without stepping on someone, except when we rolled up our mats to do exercises. The food was mostly starchy grits (which we couldn't eat), biscuits, and beans. We often found glass, bugs, and rocks in the food.

Later we were transported to the state prison where I spent the last days of my imprisonment. The food was a little better, but not much. The floor was so filthy that we had to walk through dead bugs to get into our cells. As we came in, our shoes were taken away, so we had to go barefoot. After complaining for a few days we did get our cells scrubbed and mopped. At the state prison three of us were in a cell about six feet wide and nine feet long.

In order to pass the time in jail, we scheduled various activities. First we had a quiet hour in the morning for meditation. Then we all did exercises, followed by devotions. There were Protestants, Jews, and Roman Catholics in our group, so we read from the Old and the New Testaments and also from the Catholic prayer book.

After that we conducted workshops in the practice of nonviolence and shared our experiences in nonviolent action.

We had discussions on many different topics. We took turns giving lectures on our major fields of study at school. We had talks on biology, education, economics, Greek and Roman history, and many other subjects. I found it very educational. We were able to get a few books at the county jail. When enough of us had read them we discussed the books. At the state prison, however, we had only the Bible, but there are all types of literature in the Bible.

Another thing we did to pass the time was to use bread for handicraft work. We wet the bread and molded it into various shapes—cats, dogs, and even checker and chess sets. We erased some of the letters we had received and drew checkerboards on the paper. When the guards found we had games, they let us write letters only twice a week.

We came from all parts of the country and from all walks of life, but in the prison we became one family. We had a common idea. The crowded conditions created no tensions among us. Instead we supported one another.

One night a girl in our group was telling us a Greek story. The guard told her to stop. He said we were making too much noise. She continued, so the guards took our mattresses away, and we had to sleep on the bare steel beds for three nights. During the day it was so hot we almost sweltered because the windows were closed. At night the guards opened the windows and turned on fans so that we almost froze.

One student, who had been released on an appeal bond and gone home, told her governor about conditions in the prison, so he sent a delegation to visit our group. When the visitors came, we got our mattresses back; when they left, conditions got worse again. One night several of the students had asthma attacks, but it took a long time to get medical help. When the doctor finally came he was disturbed that he had not been notified sooner; no one in authority had called him.

We found great satisfaction and inspiration in singing. We sang freedom songs and Negro spirituals as well as some popular songs. The spiritual "Nobody Knows the Trouble I've Seen" had great meaning for us. I noticed that the students who had deep religious convictions could withstand more pressure than could the agnostics or those who had religious doubts.

As a result of my participation in the freedom ride and my jail sentence, I was expelled from college at Tennessee State University, although I was later readmitted.

I grew up in the public schools of Nashville. In addition to dramatic activities, I play three instruments, paint, draw, and write poetry. I am a member of the Mount Olive Baptist Church where I was on the Youth Council and sometimes sang in the youth choir. I was baptized at the age of nine—by complete immersion as is the practice in Baptist churches.

My church helped me greatly in my decision to go on the freedom ride. The Sunday before I left I attended church and made an appeal for funds to support the effort. The people were generous with their donations. My pastor asked me if I planned to go on the freedom ride myself. I said yes. He then asked me if I would call him before I left. "I want to pray for you," he said. The night before I left on the bus I phoned him. We talked for more than an hour and his words were very encouraging. I told him I felt morally obligated to go, but my only fear was for my parents who suffered from high blood pressure. He assured me he would talk with them.

As long as I shall live, I shall always be a freedom fighter; I shall always be a participant in any struggle where any man is trying to gain the right of human dignity.

REX JORDAN is a very active layman in the Keystone
Congregational Church in Seattle, Washington

At the Gas Pump

I was changing the oil on a new Chevrolet when old George Grissum drove into the station. He is known in our neighborhood as "Gloomy George" because he always looks on the dark side of things. As a result many people avoid him as much as possible.

"Good morning, George. What can I do for you?"

"You can fix this car so it'll run, that's what you can do! I had it in here yesterday for you to work on and now it sounds worse than ever."

His belligerent tone was enough to make anybody angry. My first reaction was to remind him sharply that when he drove off it had been running smoothly. But I caught myself. Here was a lonely old man who needed someone to treat him as a human being.

"Well, drive it in here and let's have a look at it."

"You hear the way that motor's missing?" he challenged. "It never did that before."

I raised the hood and took a look around. "Here's your trouble. You just have a loose wire on one of your spark plugs." I adjusted the wire, and the motor ran smoothly.

George was quiet for a minute. "I guess that wasn't your fault, Rex. Sorry I got so hotheaded." He drove off, and there was almost a smile of appreciation on his face.

A few minutes later an expensive Buick stopped at the pump. "Hi, Rex. Fill 'er up, will you?"

"Hi, Ted. Sure thing." Ted climbed out and stood in the warm sun as I set the automatic pump and walked around to check the oil.

"Rex, how come you're always so cheerful? Don't you ever have problems like the rest of us?"

I leaned back on the fender while a quart of oil drained into the motor. I could tell from the expression on Ted's face that he was troubled about something.

"Sure I have problems, Ted. Plenty of them. And I used to let them get me down. But there came a time in my life when I realized that I couldn't solve all my problems by myself. I had to have help. At that point God became real to me for the first time in my life.

Now that I'm trying to serve God instead of myself, I still have problems, but they don't seem impossible anymore."

Ted looked at me, wonderingly.

"Do you go to church, Ted? Have you ever given God a real chance?"

"Oh, I go to church once in a while. But frankly, I don't find much in it."

"Why don't you talk with your minister about this, Ted?"

"I might," he said. Suddenly he was all business again. "How much do I owe you, Rex?" He paid me and drove off.

I was just finishing a grease job when Ed Biron walked in. "Where's your car, Ed? I don't usually see you walking."

"Out on the Everett highway, Rex. The motor went dead on me so I grabbed a bus. I thought you might be able to haul me in so you could have a look at it."

"Sure, let's go. This is as good a time as any. Hop in my truck over there. I'll be right with you." I quickly hung a sign on the door and we started up the street.

"Rex, I tried to phone you last night on another matter, but you were out. Your wife said you were speaking at some church. What was that all about?"

"Oh," I laughed. "I was holding a training session for the canvassers at Columbia Church. Art Anderson asked me to have some meetings to interpret the meaning of stewardship to their men and prepare them for their annual canvass."

"Stewardship? What's that? I'm afraid I don't speak that fancy language."

"Well, it's very simple, Ed. It means, for example, that I don't really own my station at all."

"You mean the bank owns it."

I laughed. "No, that's not exactly what I had in mind. What I meant was that *I* don't own it, *God* does. God owns my home and my car; he owns everything I have, but he has given it all to me to use during my lifetime. I am simply the steward of these possessions. I have to use them in his service, not just my own."

"So we should be grateful enough to share part of what we have with others, right?" Ed was catching on.

40

"Right! The trouble is that, human nature being what it is, we would much rather keep what we have and think we deserve more."

"Rex, you'd make a pretty good preacher." Ed thought he was kidding me.

"I am a preacher, Ed. I preach in a good many churches around the state, filling in for the minister or speaking at some special occasion. Not only that. I believe every Christian is a minister in the way he does his daily work. He's either a good one or a bad one depending on how he lives out his faith."

"Well, I'll be darned! How did you get started doing this work, Rex?"

"It was rather interesting, Ed. A few years ago I never went to church. When my boy was old enough to go to church school, I sent him off. But I knew he would soon be asking me questions I could not answer, so I followed him to church. I found they didn't have a teacher to work with the senior high young people, so I tackled that job. I learned more than they did. I found nobody was ushering at the church, either, so I started ushering at services. One day the minister took me aside and asked me if I would speak at a Laymen's Sunday service. The idea scared me, but I agreed to try it and I've never been sorry. I've found that the more I do in church work, the more it does for me. I have grown spiritually. Now my boy is married and going to college, and my daughter is in high school, and they are both active in the church."

"You know, Rex, you make religion sound more down to earth than most of the ministers I know."

"You see, Ed, I believe a man's religion begins on his job. If I can't find God at my gas pump, I won't find him at church. I think, though, that the church is a vital, basic part of every Christian's life, a cornerstone for building the kind of life God wants for us. I am in some church almost every Sunday, and I go because God's got work for us to do through his church. Everything I am, or have, or do, is created by God, and I try to dedicate all my daily life to the fulfillment of his kingdom."

"Say, there's my car up ahead, Rex. Just pull up behind it and let's have a look."

41

LILLIAN WALLACE is an active laywoman in the Shannondale
Community Church and Community Center in the Ozark
Mountains of Missouri

In Devil's Well Hollow

I stood on the front porch watching my husband Bill drive off to work. It was 5:30 in the morning, and our son was not yet awake. I paused to enjoy the quiet beauty of the morning. The sun was rising over the hill, and the mist from the river gave everything a fairyland look. I listened to the birds, watched a family of red squirrels playing on a fallen tree, and heard the sounds of farm animals awakening. It was a moment of real pleasure and beauty—another reminder that "this is my Father's world."

To me the setting for our home is picturesque and very beautiful. The house is situated on the side of a hill that rises steeply behind the house in pasture often dotted with grazing cattle. Facing the house is a steep hill covered with timber—oak, pine, and cedar—with a scattering of dogwood and redbud that furnish added beauty in the spring when they burst into glorious bloom.

I looked south down the hollow toward the river, always hung with the blue haze of Indian summer. To the north the hollow narrows, and I saw the road winding over the rolling hills always rising a little higher on the farther slopes. I was reminded of the words in the psalm:

> I lift up my eyes to the hills.
>   From whence does my help come?
> My help comes from the LORD,
>   who made heaven and earth.
>   —*Psalm 121:1*

We live on a farm in Devil's Well Hollow in the Missouri Ozarks. In the past the Ozark Mountains were famous for their "hillbillies" —colorful, poor, uneducated mountain folk. The Ozarks are still an isolated place in which to live, but the hillbilly has passed into history.

Today modern highways have replaced many of the old mountain trails, and buses transport the children to and from modern schools. Power lines reach most homes, making electric lights, radio, television, and modern plumbing available to families in the region.

43

We have a modern home with electrical appliances, television, and a large freezer filled with a variety of foods.

I grew up in Shannon County in the Ozarks and attended a one-room rural school, walking a mile and a half to get there. The schoolhouse was a new, white building nestled in a grove of pine trees, named South Shady Grove. When I started to high school I had to ride a horse two miles to the bus line, then travel about twenty miles to the school. I left home with the morning star still in the sky and returned at night with the evening star shining brightly.

For several years I taught school and attended college in the summers. After I married, I lived in California, and later in Colorado while Bill was in construction work. We spent many hours hunting, fishing, and just enjoying the beauties of the Rockies. In Colorado our son played with many different children—white, Mexican, Navajo, and Ute. They shared toys and fun, even though often each child spoke only his own language and could not understand his playmates.

One December Bill landed in the hospital with a heart condition. We were twelve hundred miles from any member of our families, and at first I felt very much alone with the heavy responsibility of a small child and the hazards of mountain winters and canyon roads. During that first day and night I suddenly realized that God was there and that *I wasn't really alone*. Some of our friends were very helpful and thoughtful. We were grateful to find that Bill had no serious ailment. My trust in God was then, and still is, a constant help to me.

Now we are back on a farm in the Ozarks where we grew up. We raise cattle and hogs. Bill still does some construction work, too. Our farm has an unusual feature called Devil's Well. There is a small opening like a well at ground level. Seventy feet underground it opens into a large cavern and an underground lake ninety feet deep.

Four miles from our farm and Devil's Well is the Shannondale Community Church and Community Center. More than twenty-five years ago our minister, the Rev. Vincent W. Bucher, began his patient work among the scattered people of this area. For many years Mr. Bucher was a traveling preacher, making the rounds to little one-room houses, fording the creeks, and preaching by the light of a coal oil lamp. By working with government groups, school boards, foresters and county agents, he has helped the area to grow. Now with better roads and more automobiles, most of his work is at the Community Center.

I grew up in the Shannondale Church where I've had many jobs, including that of church school superintendent and church organist. Bill has been on the church board and in the Men's Brotherhood.

To me, being part of the church is as natural as breathing. The church furnishes so much for all and especially for young people. Of course, Shannondale is not just a church. It is a Community Center with a program to help the people in the Ozarks learn new skills and improve their farming through such things as a church forest and strawberry field. It also provides a social and recreational program.

We learned early that the Buchers always had time for us and our problems. They gave of themselves willingly—sharing our joys and sorrows, our victories and defeats, and lending guidance and support.

For me the church and its work is a challenge—and yet it's like a tranquilizer. We are challenged to do just a little more, and to be a little better in spite of discouragement and defeat. God's love is ever present like a balm for our wounds. The church brings home to me how great is God, how beautiful his world, and how small am I.

SAMUEL DEVAPRAGASAM, a native Indian, is a minister of
the Church of South India

Filled with Joy

My name is Sam.

It's really Samuel Devapragasam (dā-vȧ-prȧ-hȧ′sŏm), but that's hard for you to pronounce. So just call me Sam. I'm a minister of the Church of South India. My parents were married in the beautiful Congregational Church at Dindigul (dĭn′dē-gŭl), and I was baptized and later ordained into the ministry there. In 1947, the Congregational, Presbyterian, Methodist, Reformed, and Anglican churches united to form the Church of South India. This historic event in the movement to bring all Christian churches together in one body made me a minister of the Church of South India.

From 1947 to 1957, I was in charge of a group of backward villages in the diocese (or district) of Madura (mȧd′ū-rȧ) and Ramnad (räm′näd). I saw some amazing things happen there. One of the most interesting was that much of the spread of the Christian faith in those villages came about *without* the work of paid ministers or missionaries.

A man from the Christian village of Mulanoor (mūl′ȧ-no͞or) married a woman from the village of Navakani (nȧ-vȧ-kŭ′nē). As the people in these two villages got to know one another, the Christian faith took root in Navakani, too. So one day I was called to Navakani to receive one hundred thirty-four people into the church. It was a day of rejoicing both for the people and the church. The moon was bright and the evening was cool, and we sat out in the open and sang praises to the Lord. Soon a minister was sent to Navakani to train the new converts and work with them.

But the villagers at Navakani did not keep their new faith to themselves. Filled with joy, they used every opportunity to tell their neighbors in the surrounding villages about this wonderful new fellowship they had found. Soon I had Christians to baptize in the nearby villages. This sharing of the faith was not done by evangelists or clergymen, but by the people in the villages.

The key village in my area was Kallimandayam (kȧl-ĭ-mȧn′thā-yȧm), and I made my headquarters there. The whole area was primitive in many respects. There were few elementary schools and no high schools. There was no medical assistance within a radius of fifteen miles, although Kallimandayam had a government doctor. Only eight people in a hundred could read and write. Poverty, filth, ignorance, superstition, disease, and death were very common.

In 1952, after six years of drought and famine in this area, many children were homeless. They wandered from village to village, their parents dead or lost. They experienced starvation, disease, and loneliness. After many months, we were able to establish an orphanage for them.

We started with twenty-eight orphans. By 1957, we had eighty-seven. The children themselves helped to make bricks and build the buildings. At the orphanage they learned to weave cloth, make soap, and work with leather. They maintained their own garden and raised chickens and sheep.

Christians in India must often face persecution and hardships from non-Christians. Some of the wealthy landowners in the Navakani area resented the fact that some of their workers were becoming Christian. So they stopped giving work to the laborers who became Christians. I went to the landowners and appealed to them to let the men work, but my words fell on deaf ears.

A month passed, and still they gave no work to the Christians. Starvation faced these men, but they remained firm in their faith. Workers from other villages were brought in to do the work, and the situation became worse. Bishop Newbigin arrived, and together we held public meetings and spoke to the non-Christians. This had no result. We left the village, saddened by the situation.

Finally, word came to me that four or five men from our congregation at Navakani were persuading the others to give up their faith in order to get work. I went to the village immediately, but I could not persuade them to change their minds. When other landowners heard how successful this method was against the Christians, they too began to put pressure on *their* Christian workers. The Christian work in all the villages was threatened with failure.

Then one day a miracle happened. A few men, who had decided to give up their faith to keep their jobs, were being taken in a procession to a local Hindu temple to proclaim before their old gods that they had given up the lordship of Christ. On the way, one of the backsliders, Kovilpillai (kō-wīl′pīl-ā), suddenly changed his mind. Kovilpillai cried out with a powerful voice, "We can never leave our Jesu Swami!" He commanded the others to march back with him.

The men's wives with other Christians had been standing some distance off, weeping and praying. The Christian group now ran toward them, shouting with joy. Together they marched back to their homes. One of the leaders came twenty-seven miles to announce the glad news to me. With my wife and other workers, I rushed to the spot, and we offered our thanks to God. This incident made a deep impression on the non-Christians, and their attitude changed. They became more friendly to us. Because this incident inspired the other Christians, the persecution gradually died out.

I have now left the Kallimandayam area to do other work in the Church of South India. The orphanage is still caring for a number of children, and the church at Kallimandayam is struggling along. Being a Christian in India means going against much of the culture, and not everyone remains faithful.[3]

DR. GLEN RICE specializes in obstetrics in Seattle, Washington

Dr. Rice Speaking

It was a pleasant Sunday morning at our house. The warm summer sun streamed in through the windows. In the distance you could see the majestic snowcapped peak of Mount Rainier looking down on the sleepy city of Seattle.

My three boys had taken charge of the morning paper and had the comics spread across the living room floor. Just as Eloise came out of the kitchen with the steaming pot of coffee in her hand, the telephone rang. She looked at me and I looked at her. For a moment neither of us moved. The phone rang again, and I slowly reached for the receiver.

"Good morning. Dr. Rice speaking."

It was Mrs. Wilton. She thought she should start for the hospital to have her baby. When she described her condition, I readily agreed with her.

"Don't rush, but I think you ought to start for the hospital fairly soon. They will take care of you until I arrive in a little while. All right? I'll see you there. Fine. Good-by." I hung up.

"It was Mrs. Wilton, dear. She's starting for the hospital in a few minutes. It looks as though I'll be delivering her child sometime this afternoon."

"I'll hurry with breakfast. Come on, boys. If we have a quick breakfast your father can drop us off at the church on the way to the hospital."

As we drove to church, I realized that I would no doubt miss the morning service that day. Somehow Sunday does not seem complete without the opportunity to meditate and worship, so I attend as often as my work will allow. I'm usually able to get to church, but occasionally a baby insists on being born at eleven o'clock on Sunday morning.

When we arrived at the church, I turned to Eloise. "I'll try to get back after church, but if I don't make it can you get a ride home with one of the neighbors?"

"Don't worry about us. We'll get home somehow."

The boys jumped out of the back seat and I drove on to the hospital. As I drove I thought about what my faith meant to me.

51

A man's faith, what he really believes, particularly at times of great stress and crisis, is to me the basis of his whole religion. During World War II, I served as a surgeon with the Marine Corps. I remember well my fears as I approached the beach in the fourth wave at Iwo Jima. Statistically, my number was up. This was my fourth landing with my battalion. Thus far I had come through almost completely unharmed. I felt that that was the day on which I might, to use the words so common then, "get it." I knew I had no more right to live than any other man in our outfit, and many men had fallen. As we churned through the water, these words went through my mind, "In everything God works for good with those who love him." (Romans 8:28) I knew that many of us would not come back from that invasion, and I felt that if I were killed it would be according to God's plan, and I would be at peace.

We are going through times now when it would be easy for any one of us to "go to pieces" if he did not have a faith that goes beyond what men can guarantee. Every day we hear someone say, "Oh, I'm terribly worried." We need to be highly concerned about many things these days if we are Christian—the threats of war among powerful nations; the inequalities involving staggering numbers of people throughout this world in their simple need for food, clothing, and shelter; and the disgraceful actions of many of us in our own country in the realm of race relations. But if we have a vital faith, we believe that with God's help these problems can be solved. We pray for guidance as to how *we* may help to find the solutions.

In times of disappointment, ill health, tragedy, and the death of loved ones, our personal faith is put to the acid test. I doubt that any one of us knows how he will measure up to those tests until the difficult times come. We must be prepared with a vital faith in a loving God. This faith cannot be secondhand—something we inherit or take for granted. Our faith must be our own, and we must trust that God is strong enough to carry us through.

I also believe that the church is the most effective instrument we have for spreading the word of God's love to all men in all places. The tremendous jobs to be done cannot be done by individuals alone. The church needs our time, our money, our thoughts, and our prayers because God has work for his church to do.

52

I particularly enjoy the Sunday church service: the quiet, the music, and the opportunity to sing. I love to sing and did a great deal of it in college, singing in both the chorus and with a quartet. I also find continual mental stimulation from the fine sermons of our minister. So often it seems that he is "pointing a finger" right at *me*, and has some of my problems and weaknesses—or hopes and dreams—in mind as he is speaking. Sometimes this makes me feel uncomfortable. More often I leave with a feeling that I can do better as a Christian and will make every effort to do so with God's help.

Arriving at the hospital, I parked my car in the lot reserved for doctors and hurried upstairs. I scrubbed my hands and put on my white gown. After I had examined Mrs. Wilton and found that she was getting along well, I decided I could make it to church after all. I left the telephone number of the church with the head nurse and told her to call me if she needed me. As I drove back to church I thought about my work as an obstetrician—a doctor who delivers babies.

For me it would be very difficult to be a sincere doctor and not be a Christian. I believe the saying is true that "the good Lord heals the patient, and we do what we can to help." I also think it would be very hard to be an atheist in the delivery room when one sees a perfect miniature specimen of the human race arrive fully equipped. I never go into the delivery room without a quickening of pulse and a sense of responsibility, no matter how many times I have been there before.

Oh yes, that afternoon Mrs. Wilton had a fine baby girl—Susan Marie!

Adlai E. Stevenson, United States representative
to the United Nations, 1960—

I believe the Christian faith has been the most significant single element in our history and our tradition. From the beginning it has been the most powerful influence in our national life. It has inspired our highest achievements.

Religious faith remains, in my opinion, our greatest national resource. It animates the great majority of our adult people. It is a very real thing to most of us. We believe that there is a Creator who has given us life and the capacity and obligation to distinguish good from evil, to serve the good and oppose the evil. We feel under a constant obligation to measure up to the highest moral purposes we know, and that in the long run the good will prove to be the wise and the practical and the lasting.

Here is the ultimate foundation beneath the strength and the security of the Republic. Here, not in our wealth, not in our productive ingenuity, not in our arms, but here in the religious convictions of our people—and in the churches in which they are nurtured—is our stability for the present and our confidence for the future.[4]

RAYMOND RODRIGUEZ grew up in the interdenominational
East Harlem Protestant Parish in New York City

"Why Aren't You Hip?"

Papo was my nickname—my real name is Raymond Rodriguez. I've lived all my life in one of the most congested slum areas in America—East Harlem in New York City.

I remember very clearly the day several years ago when I decided to become a teacher. Polly and I were co-teachers of a church school class for our church in the East Harlem Protestant Parish. We were both fifteen years old. We had a class of nine kids—Negro, Puerto Rican, and white children. Our class met in somebody's apartment because the church didn't have a classroom for us.

One Sunday we planned to have our class act out the story in Acts about Stephen who became the first Christian martyr when the crowds stoned him to death. At one point the kids were supposed to read from the Bible. Well, they just stood around. I can still remember the expressions on their faces. They looked sad and shocked, and they just didn't know what to do.

I slowly realized that they didn't know how to read! Some would read a little bit, but they were very shy and read poorly. I couldn't forget that. I wondered what they would do when they reached ninth grade and had to pass a reading test so they could graduate. But I knew that East Harlem schools were so overcrowded that the teachers couldn't give proper attention to individual pupils. I decided then to study hard and become a teacher, so I could come back and help teach kids like those.

I can understand why it is hard to get enough good teachers in East Harlem. It's extremely crowded, with as many as four thousand people living in one square block of twenty-five apartment buildings—more people in one block than live in some towns! Most of the buildings are in bad condition and should have been torn down long ago. Landlords often take advantage of the people who come from foreign countries, Puerto Rico, or the South. We must often pay enormous rents for apartments with very poor facilities. No one cleans the halls. There may not be any hot water.

Last year our apartment had no heat for five months during the coldest part of the year. The landlord just wouldn't do anything about it, even though the law requires him to. We had to keep our gas cooking stove burning all the time, but that cost too much. We had to wear sweaters in the house or cover ourselves with blankets. The East Harlem Protestant Parish organized a committee of all the tenants in the building and took the case to court. Now the landlord has sold the building, and the new landlord promises that we will have heat this winter.

The Parish has meant a lot in my life. My parents are Puerto Rican, and they belonged to the Roman Catholic Church most of their lives. When the Parish started in 1948 my mother became interested in the experiment and became a Protestant. I was raised in the Parish from the nursery up, and it has made a lot of difference to me. If it hadn't been for the Parish and my family, I might have become a member of one of the East Harlem "bopping" or fighting gangs. One of my best friends at school belonged to a gang.

One day after school he said, "Papo, why aren't you hip?"

I said, "What do you mean by *hip*?"

"You never stick around with the boys on the corner. You're not in the groove."

I thought about it. The guys on the corner spent a lot of time getting into rumbles with other gangs or picking on kids who were "different." Some of them became dope addicts or got in trouble with the law and ended up in prison. They lived by the law of the jungle. Somehow I didn't think that was right. I wasn't brought up that way, so I stayed away from the gangs.

I think ninety-seven percent of the young people in East Harlem are good kids, but the other three percent get into trouble and get so much publicity that they give the rest of us a bad name. This is rough because it means we have two strikes against us before we begin.

Sometimes before saying or doing anything I stop and think: what does the church have to say about this? I remember one time on my way to high school with a friend when he said, "Let's cut classes and go to a movie!"

We had been going to that school for only two weeks and the homework was already heavy, but I was tempted. Then I thought of my parents and how they were really making a sacrifice so we kids could go to school—I have six brothers and sisters. And I thought of the Parish. I remembered all that the ministers had done to give me moral support and encouragement to go on to school. I went to class that day.

The East Harlem Protestant Parish did a lot to help us. The ministers and their families lived in our neighborhood, so we really got to know them. Most of the Protestant churches had moved out of East Harlem before the Parish moved into a storefront office and began reaching out to people. The East Harlem Protestant Parish was sponsored by several denominations working together. In addition to church school and worship services, the Parish had a special program to help drug addicts and a program to help kids learn to read better. The Parish tried to help us in many ways. I guess I'm lucky I grew up in the East Harlem Protestant Parish.

SOSHICHIRO SASAKI was a kamikaze (suicide) pilot for Japan during World War II. Now a Christian, he is an agricultural specialist among underprivileged people in the Iwate Mountains

Alive Today

I opened my eyes and looked into the kind face of a nurse bending over me. I was in a large room with many beds, all occupied by men. I was very weak, but I felt grateful to be alive. I could remember the blinding explosion that had struck our ship on the way from Japan to the China coast—that was almost the last thing I did remember. We had been on our way to our assignments as kamikaze (käm-ĭ-käz′ē) pilots—suicide pilots who would dive-bomb their planes into enemy ships to destroy them.

"Where am I?" I asked faintly.

"You are in a veterans' hospital in Japan," the nurse replied.

"The war? How is it going?" I was almost afraid to ask the fateful question.

"The war is over. Japan surrendered some time ago."

Disappointment and bitterness swept over me. Those hated Americans! So they had won. Now the world was at their mercy.

Some time later a doctor came to examine me.

"Doctor, what is my condition? Tell me honestly."

"Since you want to know, I'll tell you. You came here in a state of complete physical collapse. You had what we thought was a hopeless case of tuberculosis. Fortunately we now have received drugs that should cure you before long."

He drew a wicked-looking needle from his bag and gave me an injection of medicine from a small bottle. After he had left I examined the empty bottle. The label indicated that the medicine had come from the United States. "That's strange," I thought. "Why should the bloodthirsty Americans send medicine to a conquered land?"

I asked the nurse about it. "Yes, it's true," she said. "Without the food and medicine sent from America you would not be alive today, nor would many other Japanese."

"But they taught us during the war that Americans are cruel, inhuman, and bloodthirsty. That's why I left Agricultural College in Tokyo to become a suicide pilot."

The nurse smiled. "Of course there are Americans like that. But there are some cruel people right here in Japan too."

I determined to learn more about the Americans so I would know the truth. After all, their medicine had saved my life. At the same time I decided to act on an old Japanese custom—I would commit suicide rather than submit to the humiliation of living in a defeated nation.

Soon after this I looked up and saw the nurse approaching with a smile on her face. "You have visitors," she said. Behind her were my wife Mitsuko-san (mĭt-sū′kō-sän) and our little boy. A big lump came to my throat as I joyfully greeted them.

I learned later that the food and medicine that had come from America had been sent largely because of the inspiration of Christian teachings. "Love your enemy" was a Christian teaching, I discovered. With gratitude toward my former enemies, I asked my wife to inquire further about Christianity at a nearby church. I decided to postpone my suicide until I could learn more about the Christian faith. My wife returned with a Bible and some Christian literature.

I was so impressed with Christianity that when I was discharged from the hospital after an operation some time later, my wife and I became Christians. I became the youngest elder of the church we joined—the same church Mitsuko-san had gone to for the Bible and literature. For several years, while my health was still weak, my wife and I ran a small stationery store, but it was barely enough to keep us going.

Then came a great day. I received word that I had been awarded a scholarship from the United States to complete my studies at the Agricultural College in Tokyo. So I returned to school while Mitsuko-san stayed behind at home to work. I finished my master's degree in the spring of 1956, and a difficult decision was forced upon me. I was offered a position as an instructor at the college because I had been an outstanding student. This position would bring honor to me and to my family. At the same time I had an opportunity to take a very hard and low-paying job working for the Christian churches of Japan. They needed a man of my background to work in the mountain areas, teaching the poor farmers how to make better use of their meager farmlands. I decided on the church job.

During the spring, summer, and fall of 1956, I tramped the hills with Paul R. Gregory, a missionary of the Evangelical and Reformed Church. We held training courses for groups of farmers in straw-thatched homes, in tumbledown mountain schoolhouses, and occasionally in Buddhist temples. These people were still suffering from the famine years of 1954–1956. We taught them how to plant clover seed and rotate their crops to make better use of the land. We taught them how to raise dairy animals so they would no longer rely on their rice crop alone. As we worked in the mountains I also found opportunities to speak of the complete change in my life that the Christian faith had made.

Later Mitsuko-san, our son, and I were put in charge of a new cattle breeding center in the heart of the Iwate Mountains. We did some experimental farming and breeding of dairy cattle with the help of Church World Service and the Heifer Project, Inc.

Part of the work that we liked especially was the training program. We often had groups of ten or twelve boys from farm families at our center. They stayed for weeks or even months at a time. I taught them a concentrated course in agriculture and dairying. If young boys can learn how to be better farmers, it may prevent in the future the kind of famine that has taken so many lives in the past.

My family and I also have had opportunity to share with these boys the Christian faith that has made life so rich and full of meaning for us.

Lyndon B. Johnson, President of the United States, 1963–

My fellow Americans:

Only yesterday I went before the Congress to speak for the first time as President of the United States. Tonight, on this Thanksgiving, I come before you to ask your help, to ask your strength, to ask your prayers that God may guard this republic and guide my every labor . . .

It is this work that I most want us to do—to banish rancor from our words and malice from our hearts—to close down the poison springs of hatred and intolerance and fanaticism—to perfect our unity North and South, East and West, to hasten the day when bias of race, religion and region is no more and to bring the day when our great energies, and decencies and spirit will be free of the burden that we have borne too long. . . .

On this Thanksgiving Day as we gather in the warmth of our families, in the mutual love and respect which we have for one another and as we bow our heads in submission to divine Providence, let us also thank God for the years that He gave us inspiration through His servant.

Let us today renew our dedication to the ideals that are American. Let us pray for His divine wisdom in banishing from our land any injustice or intolerance or oppression to any of our fellow Americans, whatever their opinion, whatever the color of their skins, for God made all of, not some of, us in His image.

All of us, not just some of us, are His children.

—from his Thanksgiving Day address,
November 28, 1963.

WILLIAM H. GLASER was a streetcar conductor and bus driver in St. Louis, Missouri, for thirty-six years

View from a Bus

I pulled my bus up to the corner and slowly came to a stop. A lady about eighty years old was standing at the corner with a large package beside her. I set the brakes and hopped off.

"Good morning, Mrs. Reardon."

"Good morning, Mr. Glaser. How are you today?"

"I'm just fine, thank you. And isn't it a beautiful day?"

I took Mrs. Reardon's arm and helped her up the steps. Every Tuesday and Thursday Mrs. Reardon was at the same corner, waiting to take the bus to see her daughter on the other side of town. Her daughter wasn't well, and she usually took some baked goods or canned food along when she went. I picked up the package from the sidewalk and set it down beside Mrs. Reardon when she took her seat near the front of the bus.

As the bus started down the street, she said, "You don't know how much older people appreciate a little help. I know you must be a Christian by the way you treat us."

It made me feel warm inside to hear those simple words of appreciation. "Yes, as a matter of fact I am a Christian, Mrs. Reardon. I've been a church school teacher for many years. I still teach a class of junior high boys. I think it's very important to belong to a church. And those youngsters keep me young too; they really keep me on my toes."

Three or four people boarded the bus at the next stop. As the passengers sat down, I noticed that one of them took the seat directly behind my driver's seat. I turned to him with a smile and said, "I wonder if you would mind taking a seat farther back in the bus. I have to save that seat for one of my regular passengers." He didn't seem to mind and quickly took another seat. At the next stop a blind man with his Seeing-Eye dog got on.

"Good morning, Bill," he said as he climbed aboard.

"How are you this morning, John? Hi, Pal."

He took the seat I had reserved for him. I've picked up John every morning and taken him to work for years. He has seldom had to grope for a seat on the crowded bus when I'm his driver. His dog, Pal, and I have become good friends too. Pal always sat be-

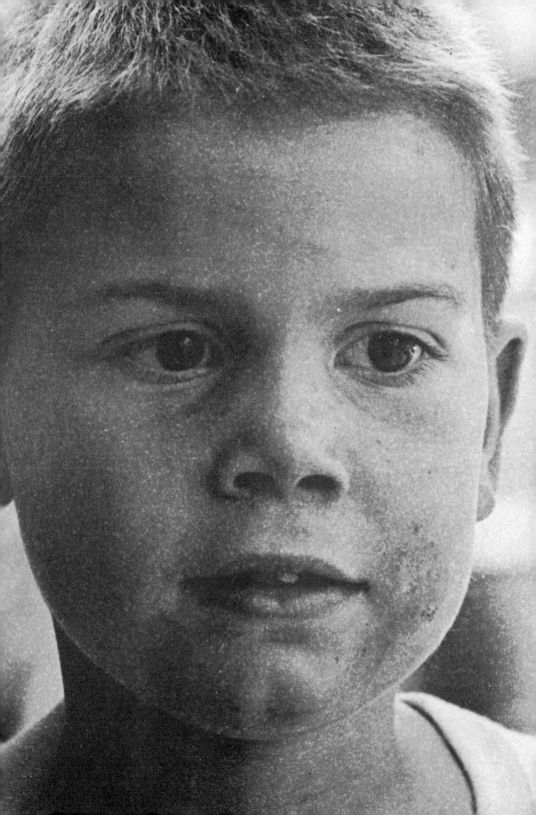

side his master and rested his head on his lap for the trip downtown. Both John and his dog usually knew when we had reached their stop, but if they were unsure I would remind them, "Here's your stop. Have a good day at work." And I've always made sure they crossed the street safely before I started up again.

We drove on through the crowded part of town, and several young people got up and offered their seats to older people. I have seen this kind of courtesy every day, although occasionally some people have stayed selfishly in their seats while older persons or pregnant women stood. In my work I've met people of all kinds and of every race and background. As a Christian I believe in being kind and considerate to everyone.

A little boy climbed on. Several tears were tracing their way through the dirt on his cheeks.

"What's the matter, son?"

"I lost my money. How can I get home?"

"That's all right, son. You sit down right here and we'll see that you get home."

I dug a dime out of my pocket and put it in the fare box. "I'll pay your fare this time and you can send it to me later. Just send it to Bill Glaser in care of the bus company, and I'll get it OK."

When he got off he was still sniffling a little, but he was a happier boy. I have often had opportunities to help people who have lost their fare or forgotten their pocketbooks. About half the people sent the money back, and I think that's pretty good.

I saw that we had reached Mrs. Reardon's corner, but she was daydreaming and had not noticed where we were. "Mrs. Reardon, here's your stop," I said quietly.

She started a bit, and smiled as she stepped from the bus cautiously. As I handed her package down to her, she said, "Thanks so much. See you Thursday." I nodded and drove on.

You can see that I believe our Christian faith works on the job. In my thirty-seven years driving streetcars and buses in St. Louis, I have found many ways to be a Christian. You can help people in the little ways, whether you are driving a bus, working in an office, or doing anything else. I think helping people is a big part of being Christian.

JIMILU MASON is an artist and sculptor in Washington, D.C.

Talent to Bring Joy

I had been working patiently and carefully. The damp clay felt good in my hands. A strong face was beginning to emerge from the formless shape before me. I had entered the most important competition of my career as a serious artist, and one more day would reveal whether or not my weeks of work had been worth the effort.

The Supreme Court of the United States wanted a marble bust of the late Chief Justice Vinson. When I heard of it, I decided to enter the competition. Three other sculptors had already submitted models. I had worked for weeks on the likeness, and the result of my efforts was in sight. The next morning the Vinson family was coming to see my model and pass judgment on it.

I worked late that night, and as the evening wore on I began to get anxious. The expression on the model just did not seem to want to come alive. The more anxious I became, the faster the likeness drifted away. I seemed to be having more and more difficulty. I glanced at my watch and was horrified to discover that it was nearly midnight. I was almost in tears. Would all my work be in vain because time had run out?

I worked feverishly for several more hours, but I got nowhere. The inner spark I wanted simply would not come. I was completely exhausted. I took my tool and drove it into the clay figure. In despair I said, "All right, God, if you're so great you do it!" It was my honest prayer for help. I went to bed regretting that I had not really prayed as I should have before starting this work. I had not offered up my talent to God.

The next morning I was up early and in just a few hours the whole expression just fell into place. When the family arrived to see the model, I knew it was good. Mrs. Vinson sat for a long time before the bust in silence. As she looked at the figure of her deceased husband, tears filled her eyes. The members of the family soon agreed that they would recommend that the Supreme Court accept my entry. I was overjoyed; I could hardly believe it was true. As I prayed that night I gave thanks to God, not just that I had won the commission, but that he had given me the talent to be an artist—a talent I could use to bring joy to myself and others.

I soon learned that the members of the Supreme Court were reluctant to grant the commission to a young and unknown sculptor such as I, but they were finally persuaded. Today my white marble bust of Chief Justice Frederick Moore Vinson stands in the entrance hall of the Supreme Court Building in Washington, D.C.

I had become a sculptor almost without being aware of it. During high school and college years I assumed I would continue as a painter. However, one day some friends asked me to do a bust of their daughter. Although I had studied sculpture, at first I refused. I just was not interested. Finally I yielded to their persuasion, and the bust turned out quite well. They told some of their friends how pleased they were and I was soon on my way to becoming a professional sculptor.

One of the greatest thrills of my life came the day I was called to the White House to do a bust of President Lyndon B. Johnson. It was hard work to get him to sit still long enough for me to work on a model. There were always secretaries running in and out, but I shall never forget the experience.

At about the time I began to work seriously as a sculptor, I became associated with an unusual institution, the Church of the Saviour. At dinner one evening a friend spoke about this church with such enthusiasm that I began to inquire.

"Where is the church located?" I asked.

"Well, the members don't have a regular church building," she replied. "They have their meetings and offices in an old brownstone house on Massachusetts Avenue."

"How large is the membership, then?" I inquired. "It couldn't be too big if they meet in an old house."

"The actual membership averages seventy members, but there are many people exploring membership and many more who just come to worship on Sunday."

"I don't understand. Why doesn't the church take everybody who wants to join?"

"You see, these people feel that most churches are too large and people hardly know one another. This is just one way they take their Christian faith seriously."

"What denomination is it—Methodist or what?"

72

BUST OF FREDERICK MOORE VINSON   Jimilu Mason

"It doesn't belong to any one denomination; it is an ecumenical church."

I became more and more interested the more I heard about this unusual church. I decided to visit it. One Friday night I attended its School for Christian Living. The evening began with a supper, followed by a period of worship and classes on the Bible and various aspects of Christian faith. I was immediately impressed by the genuineness of the people. They really cared about me, whereas the impression many churches gave me was that I was just the 507th member. At the Church of the Saviour the warmth was very magnetic and just drew me into it, as into a family.

I decided I wanted to belong to that fellowship. However, I soon learned that it was not that easy. Before I could become a member I had to go through a two-year period of study and preparation under the guidance of a member of the church who acted as my sponsor. I had to study seriously the meaning of Christian beliefs and the principles of the Christian life, as well as the Bible. I had to learn to discipline my life through a period of daily prayer and Bible study and to understand the real meaning and importance of worship. For a person to whom church had been simply a Sunday appointment, this was a radical change. And that was not all.

Every member of the Church of the Saviour agrees to practice tithing, contributing *at least* ten percent of his income. We feel that this is the smallest amount a Christian should share with others in gratitude to God for all he has given us. In addition, each member of the church undertakes some specific task for the church. I taught the third and fourth grade in our church school as one of my tasks.

One of the most interesting things I have done was to work one night a week in the Potter's House, a unique coffee house sponsored by the church. If you visit the Potter's House, you will find a dimly-lit room with some paintings displayed on the wall. People from many walks of life—students and working people, young and old—come to have refreshments and talk.

The waiters and waitresses are members or friends of the Church of the Saviour. We talk with some of the people who want to talk; others prefer to be left alone. Some people ask about the church;

others are not interested. In this way the church tries to meet average people who usually do not come to churches. We tried to help some; we listened and learned from others.

On the nights when I worked, I met at 6:45 with my regular group of fellow workers. We had some time together in prayer. Then we discussed some of the people who might come in that night, and how we might be open to listen to their problems, to help them, and just to love them. We talked about some of the people who were hard to love and how we might understand them better. Then we received our assignments for the night—dishwasher, waiter, hostess, busboy, cashier. At eight o'clock the doors would open and usually we were engulfed for four hours in a unique effort to make the church come alive for the lonely, lost people of the world, or those who had simply written the church off as irrelevant.

On the wall of the Potter's House hangs one of my favorite sculptures, entitled "Saint Peter After the Denial." It is my effort to portray Peter in his agony after denying that he knew Jesus. It is an attempt to interpret personal insight through art.

Since joining the Church of the Saviour I have come to know that we really can't do anything without God, once we dedicate and commit our lives to him. As an artist I can take no credit for anything good that I do; it comes straight from God. We who are members of the Church of the Saviour know that we are no better than anyone else. We are simply trying to help one another take seriously what the Christian faith is all about and to commit our lives as fully as we can to Christ.

Dwight D. Eisenhower, retired five-star General and Chief of Staff, United States Army. President of the United States, 1953–1961

We put our faith in the love of God and neighbor. This faith provides the indispensable base for true self-government; on it is based our dedication to the rights and dignity of man. It includes our loyalty to those qualities of life which are uppermost in the Christian tradition: justice, charity, peace, and the truth that sets men free. These qualities—these spiritual values—are taught and defended by the church. In the exercise of them, and in the full use of our God-given talents—be they in education, industry, government, or the arts—each person freely finds his highest fulfillment.[5]

77

DR. WILLIAM L. NUTE, SR., served for nearly a half-century as a medical missionary in Turkey

Doctor on Horseback

It was a strange feeling to stand in the airport in Istanbul ready to leave Turkey for the last time. Forty-five years of my life had been devoted to the people of that land. For Mary, my wife, standing beside me, it had been fifty-one years. Now we were "retired missionaries" on our way to Switzerland for a short vacation, then on to England, and finally to America.

I thought back to the day when I had stood with my graduating class at Yale forty-five years before. Then I recalled my assignment to teach in Tarsus, the birthplace of the apostle Paul. That's where I met Mary and we became husband and wife.

After three years in Tarsus as a teacher for the American Board (now the United Church Board for World Ministries), I knew that I wanted to spend my life in Turkey. So back to the United States I came for seven years of medical training. When I returned to Turkey to stay, I came as a medical missionary. I was *Dr.* Nute rather than *Mr.* Nute.

Waiting for our plane in Istanbul, I thought of the little clinic we had just left in Talas (tà-läs). In my mind I relived a typical day in that clinic where I had worked so many years.

I rose with the sun and looked out my bedroom window. Sure enough, the patients were already gathering. Some were arriving on foot; others rode in carts, or were carried on stretchers by their friends. There were patients with every kind of problem—a child whose feet had been badly burned by boiling tea and who also suffered from measles and pneumonia; a young couple with five children, both parents suffering from tuberculosis; an old lady with cancer. Our nurses worked hard cleaning up the patients, preparing them for physical examinations, and giving treatments. My wife, Mary, helped by interviewing patients, keeping records, and giving much needed advice and comfort.

Some of the patients could pay a modest fee, while others showed their gratitude by bringing gifts of milk, eggs, or yogurt. It was truly touching and heart-warming. Always one of the hardest tasks of the day was turning away the fifteen or twenty patients who had to be put on a waiting list!

One night after the clinic we wearily sat down for supper. We had just begun to eat when it was announced that another patient had arrived. At first I said I simply could not see anyone else that day. The clinic was closed, the nurses had gone home, the place had been cleaned up, and the instruments had been put away.

Then I discovered that the patient was a critically ill baby. I went down to the steet to talk to the mother. She had taken the baby to a doctor in the city, but he had said the baby would die and did nothing for her. In desperation, the mother had brought her to our clinic. I examined the baby and found that there was little hope. I did all I could for her, and asked the mother to bring her back early in the morning. I learned later that the baby had recovered and the mother was very grateful.

Once or twice a week I closed the clinic early and started on a trip to the villages. There were patients in hundreds of out-of-the-way villages who could not get to the clinic and who had no doctors. I stuffed some sandwiches into my coat pockets, put my heavy pack of instruments and medical supplies on my back, saddled my horse, and climbed into the saddle. Behind me was my "yamche" (yäm-chä), a great, heavy, felt shepherd's cloak.

A heavy wind was blowing across the plateau from the southwest as I left the clinic one afternoon. I knew it would be a hard trip if the wind did not die down by sundown. I soon left the main road and began climbing up a rocky canyon. I looked back and saw the mission school and the clinic I had left behind at Talas. In the distance the snowcapped mountain peaks were visible. I was headed for Kuru Kopru (koo-roo kŏ-proo), a village of one hundred-fifty homes. It would take me about two hours on horseback. The road, if one could call it that, was very difficult to follow, and I recalled the dark night I had lost the road entirely and wandered for hours in a snowstorm.

I arrived at the first village with its low, flat-roofed, brownstone hovels and an occasional two-story house nestled against the foot of the cliffs in a narrow canyon. I could hear the familiar call, "Doktor geliyor!" (The doctor is coming!) going through the village from house to house. A crowd quickly gathered as I reined up in front of a house where I knew there was sickness.

80

I dismounted and entered the gate. Inside was a small courtyard and a door leading into the house beyond. All but about six feet of the house was a cave dug into the cliff. Just inside the door was a fireplace with a pile of twigs burning on it. Five or six ragged children huddled on quilts before the fire. I led my horse into the house and through into the cave beyond, leaving him there with the family cattle. A kerosene lamp provided some light. In one corner of the cave was a large storage bin for grain.

When I had finished with the patient there, I went to another home nearby. Then I saw several of the village children in a make-shift "clinic" at a "rich" man's home. When I had finished and was riding out of the village, a man came running alongside my horse.

"Please come and see my daughter-in-law."

"But I have no more time."

"She is very sick."

"All right, just this once . . ."

And so it went. There was no end to the patients needing help. I ate my sandwiches as I rode on to the next village. It had turned quite cold, and the wind was blowing harder than ever, driving rain into my face. Once my horse slipped on the wet stones of a steep incline and tumbled me off. I was not hurt, and quickly re-mounted. One more village stop and I was on my way home, eager for a few hours sleep before beginning again at dawn with the usual rounds of the Talas clinic.

I remember one stormy night when I was returning from a village trip and lost my way. I wandered for several hours in a thick vineyard, losing my glasses in the process. The next day I retraced my path, following the hoofmarks in the mud, but I could not find the hard-to-replace glasses. When the people in the nearest village heard about it, the men and boys swarmed out to look for them. Hours later they found the glasses hanging from a tree, unbroken.

On Sunday mornings we worshiped with our fellow missionaries. On Sunday evenings we had a simple service of worship in our home with twenty-five or thirty Turkish Christians who came to be with us. There was no Christian church in Talas, although there had been years before.

Was it worth all the difficulties? Without a hospital it sometimes seemed hopeless. Once, as if to renew my faith, a woman I
had seen eight years before came in. She had been suffering from
tuberculosis then, but now she looked healthy and rosy-cheeked.
Although the X-rays showed that there was still a little infection,
she had followed my advice and was doing well. She was full of
gratitude for the help she had found at the clinic.

Was being a missionary in Turkey worthwhile?

I must say an emphatic "Yes." Of course there were difficulties
and limitations, but they were not really important. What was
important, was that the love of Christ spoke to men through us.
When I left, a former student traveled across the Taurus Mountains
to thank me because years before a word from me had set him on a
path of distinguished service to his fellow Turks. A woman also
came, bringing a parting gift and saying through her tears that
Allah through me had saved her child's life. And well I remember
the man whom I did not know who, unasked, shouldered my
saddlebag and broke a way for me through the snow.

In Turkey we tried to serve our Lord Jesus Christ and to be
true to the vision of the worldwide extent and complete oneness
of the kingdom of God on earth.[6]

HAROLD GOLDTHWAITE, an apple grower, is an active
layman in the Evangelical Congregational Church of
Dunstable, Massachusetts

The Gift of God

It was a chill September morning, and the sun had just appeared over the green, wooded hills of Massachusetts when I finished breakfast. I pulled on my sweater and hurried out to the loaded truck in the barn. In the soft light of the early morning I could see the dew glistening on the grass, and it reminded me that the first frost was not far away. The motor coughed and sputtered for a few minutes, then settled into a steady hum as it warmed up.

I drove the forty miles into Boston with my precious load of farm-fresh vegetables and apples. Especially apples. I'm an apple grower, and the bushels of beautiful, crisp, red apples on the back of the truck were evidence of my season's work. I pulled the truck up to the curb at an open-air market. I had barely begun to set up a display of fruit and vegetables before people were crowding around the truck.

"I'll have some of this squash, please."

"Give me five pounds of those big tomatoes."

"Can you sell me a bushel of McIntosh apples this morning?"

With modern supermarkets there aren't many places where open-air markets still survive, but I have been coming to this same spot for years. The faces of many of my customers were familiar. The place is just a block from the hill where George Washington's troops fired on the British ships as they sailed out of Boston Harbor in the Revolutionary War.

As the crowds gathered from all over the neighborhood, I remembered to set aside some apples and vegetables for one faithful old customer who was now confined to her home. I would stop by her house on the way out of town and deliver her order.

"I'll have some green beans, three pounds of tomatoes, and a bag of those Cortland apples."

"Ten pounds of apples here."

The customers continued to come, and I worked as fast as I could. One lady asked for a dollar's worth of apples. As I handed her the heavy bag, she thrust a five dollar bill into my hand and turned to hurry off. "Wait a minute," I called. "You gave me a five."

"Oh," she said, "so I did. Thank you very much."

I gave her four ones in change. In my work there is always the temptation to cut corners and take unfair advantage of people at times, but I find that strict honesty and fair dealing is not only easier but better paying in the long run. Perhaps the Golden Rule— do unto others as you would have them do unto you—describes how I believe in applying my religion in my daily work. I try to use this rule in dealing with my customers and the people who work for me.

Going to market is just one of the many parts of my work. I have about twenty-five acres in apple orchards, and during the fall harvest season I keep ten or twelve people busy picking the crop.

But my work doesn't end when all the apples are picked. Some of the crop is sold immediately, but most of it goes into cold storage. During the winter I deliver apples to my regular customers— small grocery stores in Nashua, New Hampshire, just over the state line.

In addition to selling, sorting, and packing apples during the winter, the trees have to be pruned. So I manage to keep busy most of the year.

It is a pleasure to work in an occupation where I come in contact with growing things and realize the great goodness and bounty of God. Have you ever seen an apple orchard in blossom in the spring? Beauty like that is one of God's great gifts to us.

Across the street from my home is the white frame building of the only church in town—the Evangelical Congregational Church. We have about one hundred fifty members, and the church is usually served by a student minister who attends one of the seminaries in the Boston area. I've been a member of that church most of my life—since I came here as a young deacon. Many times through the years I have served communion to our small congregation. I attend meetings of the Men's Club, and help with the ushering when I'm needed. I'm also a member of a planning committee, preparing for the future growth of our church. I've even tried my hand at preaching—on Laymen's Sunday one year.

I belong to the church because I believe it is the least we can do when all that we have and all that we are is the gift of God.

The church means a tie with the spiritual forces in the world, trying to make it a better place in which to live. I get inspiration from the Sunday services, and in the church I find the companionship of others who are trying to live good lives. Regular attendance at church school and morning worship gives me something that no other association does—I realize that I belong to God's family on earth.

I think possibly we Protestants take the church too much for granted. I think we need more participation by families. God loves us as his family; in the church our human families can give thanks for his love and share it with others.

ALBERT JENKINS, engineer of a diesel locomotive, helped
to develop the Milliron retreat grounds of the Mt. Zion and Grace
Evangelical and Reformed Churches near Pittsburgh

Where You Find God

Joe and I were lying on our backs in the dirt under the old church. We were right under the ancient log beam that held up the crumbling floor, and we were slowly turning the handles on two big truck jacks. We had to lift the whole building enough to put in railroad ties where the rotting supports used to be. It gave me the jitters to hear the walls creak and groan every time we gave the jacks a turn. But when we crawled out from under the building, we felt good. This old chapel which we were rebuilding for our parish retreat grounds was actually beginning to take shape.

Some of the happiest days of my life have been spent these past few summers at our Milliron retreat grounds. Ever since the two congregations—Mt. Zion in West Mifflin and Grace Church in Duquesne—started the project, I have found that going to church is more than a once-a-week affair. It's a matter of really *being* together to do something for God.

When you spend hours rubbing shoulders with your fellow church members hacking a new picnic grove out of the wilderness, helping a friend build his cabin, or digging out a spring-hole, you really get to know people and feel the excitement of serving the Lord in a fresh, new way.

Families were brought together, too, at our retreat grounds. I'll never forget the first night we tented out on our family lot at Milliron, listening to the dogs barking as they chased a fox on the hill above us! And how Buddy, Pat, Joan, Sandy, and my wife, Helen, pitched in to help build our cozy cabin. The whole church was a family too, when we all sat quietly at the evening services in the chapel we had all helped to rebuild. Other times we rocked the walls with hymn singing that would have matched that of the pioneers who once worshiped on the same spot.

The site of our retreat grounds has had some historic associations. The Milliron church dates back to 1793 when John William Weber, the Reformed Church's pioneer missionary, settled here in western Pennsylvania. The rebuilt chapel, which we now use for our family vesper services on Sunday evenings in July and August, is named the Weber Memorial Chapel.

In future years we hope to have a lake and picnic grove on the retreat grounds as well as family cabins like ours. It has been a thrilling experiment in which our parish life has been enriched by shared labor and retreat.

Don't get me wrong, though. There is much more to church for me than our Milliron retreat project. Seven years ago when my family joined Mt. Zion Evangelical and Reformed Church, church-going was just a habit for us. Now I really look forward to it. The Milliron experiment has helped me appreciate my own church more. I understand now that the church is really interested in a man and can make a difference in his life. It's our job in the church to help others to realize this is true. I guess that's why I'm so interested in the visitation program of my church. I'm not much of a talker, but on the visits we make to strangers and lazy members I try to tell people what the church has meant to me and my family. I think that because I've spent my life working with my hands, however, I can do more good by doing than talking.

When our Churchmen's Brotherhood builds a new wall, or moves furniture, or shovels slag for the parking lot, I make it a point to be on hand. A mission church in a small town needs a lot of strong backs. It needs strong thinking and praying too. Having just been elected a deacon, I see more and more the struggles and sacrifices that are necessary to keep the church doing its job in the world.

My wife and I try to train our children to see how much the work of the church needs them. I'm proud that they are all with us in church every Sunday and that our oldest daughter is already an assistant church school teacher.

Christianity has to reach out beyond the doors of Mt. Zion Church, and I try to practice my Christian faith on the job. Believe me, it's not easy. Since I work in a steel mill, I see human nature in the raw. I work the 11 P.M. to 7 A.M. shift at the J. & L. Works in Pittsburgh, operating a diesel locomotive. We haul molten iron from the blast furnace—ninety tons in each big ladle—to the open hearth where it is burned to make steel.

As an engineer I've had a lot of experiences. There are plenty of opportunities to live your Christianity. For example, take "Big

90

Georch" and his umbrella. "Big Georch" was hired as a brake-man during the war. He had a lot of strange old-country ways and could hardly speak a word of English, so the boys really gave him a hard time. One rainy night he showed up at work with a big black umbrella and hoisted it over his head as he walked along the tracks throwing switches. When I saw that I grabbed my own raincoat from the cab and rushed it out to him. I figured he would either be killed by some train he couldn't see for the obstruction, or laughed off the job by the boys. They were just waiting for him to do something crazy anyway. After all, when you have "the league of nations" working together as we did in our place, you have to give a man a break and try to get along with everyone.

When I wonder about the big problems of the world I can't help thinking that Christianity can really make a difference. The church can show the way by being a place where people learn to live to-gether, regardless of whether they have dirt under their finger-nails or their name is Bolinski. Through the church, too, you can put to work the strength and know-how the Lord gave you for the benefit of your fellowmen. And in the church service you have time to think, and are forced to think about the things you do that you should not do and those you don't do that you should. In worship is where you find God, who will take you back when you fail and straighten you out again.[7]

Footnotes and Acknowledgments

1. Based on a story in *The Winnebago Finds a Friend* by Arthur V. Casselman. Heidelberg Press, Philadelphia, 1944. Used by permission of The Christian Education Press. Also from material in a letter to the author from Benjamin Stucki, dated September 28, 1960. The story is written as if Mr. Stacy had written it himself.
2. Excerpts from "Letter from a Birmingham Jail" by Martin Luther King, Jr., from *The Christian Century*, June 12, 1963 issue. Copyright 1963, Christian Century Foundation. Reprinted by permission. Also by permission of Martin Luther King, Jr.
3. Adapted in part from *Kallimandayam Diary* by Sam. Devapragasam. Lenox Press, Pasumalai, India, 1958.
4. From a letter to the author from Elinor Green, public relations officer, United States Mission to the United Nations, November 1, 1961.
5. From a letter to the author from Frederic Fox, Special Assistant in the White House, August 24, 1960.
6. Adapted from "I'm the Doctor" by Lloyd Swift and from other material of the United Church Board for World Ministries.
7. Written in large part by the Rev. Gabriel Fackre for the author from information supplied to Mr. Fackre by Albert Jenkins.